DK READERS

4 READERS

Snow Dogs!
Racers of the North

Written by Ian Whitelaw

DK Publishing

On the frozen trail

Bone-numbing cold
During the 1973 Iditarod race, the temperature dropped to –60°F (–51°C), and with a strong wind blowing it felt much colder than that!

Imagine the feeling. You are in the middle of nowhere, rushing through an Arctic landscape of forests, mountains, rivers of ice, and endless white. Your sled runners hiss against the snow, and your face tingles in a shower of sparkling ice crystals thrown up by the speeding dogs. You guide your sled along the trail's swoops and dips, shouting encouragement to your team of huskies.

A Note to Parents

DK READERS is a compelling program for beginning readers, designed in conjunction with leading literacy experts, including Dr. Linda Gambrell, Professor of Education at Clemson University. Dr. Gambrell has served as President of the National Reading Conference, the College Reading Association, and the International Reading Association.

Beautiful illustrations and superb full-color photographs combine with engaging, easy-to-read stories to offer a fresh approach to each subject in the series. Each DK READER is guaranteed to capture a child's interest while developing his or her reading skills, general knowledge, and love of reading.

The five levels of DK READERS are aimed at different reading abilities, enabling you to choose the books that are exactly right for your child:

Pre-level 1: Learning to read
Level 1: Beginning to read
Level 2: Beginning to read alone
Level 3: Reading alone
Level 4: Proficient readers

The "normal" age at which a child begins to read can be anywhere from three to eight years old. Adult participation through the lower levels is very helpful for providing encouragement, discussing storylines, and sounding out unfamiliar words.

No matter which level you select, you can be sure that you are helping your child learn to read, then read to learn!

LONDON, NEW YORK, MUNICH,
MELBOURNE, AND DELHI

Editor Julia Roles
U.S. Editor John Searcy

Reading Consultant
Linda Gambrell, Ph.D.

Produced by
Shoreline Publishing Group LLC
Editorial Director James Buckley, Jr.
Designer Tom Carling, carlingdesign.com

First American Edition, 2008
Published in the United States by DK Publishing
375 Hudson Street, New York, New York 10014

Copyright © 2008 Dorling Kindersley Limited

Dorling Kindersley is represented in Canada by
Tourmaline Editions Inc
662 King Street West, Suite 304
Toronto, Ontario M5V 1M7

DK books are available at special discounts when purchased in bulk
for sales promotions, premiums, fund-raising, or educational use.
For details, contact: DK Publishing Special Markets, 375 Hudson
Street, New York, New York 10014, or SpecialSales@dk.com

A catalog record for this book
is available from the Library of Congress.

ISBN: 978-0-7566-4081-1 (Paperback)
ISBN: 978-0-7566-4082-8 (Hardcover)

Printed and bound in China by L. Rex Printing Co., Ltd

08 09 10 11 12 10 9 8 7 6 5 4 3 2 1

The publisher would like to thank the following for their kind
permission to reproduce their photographs:
(b = bottom; c = center; t = top; l = left; r = right)
All photos by Jeff Schultz/Alaska Stock Images except the following:
AGE Fotostock: 34tl; AP/Wide World: 23tr, 24bl; Blue Sky
Productions: 30tl, 32c, 34bl, 35tr, 38l, 45tr; Tom Carling: 22tl;
Canadian Museum of Civilization: 12tl; Corbis: 13t;
Dreamstime.com: 10tl, 21br, 39tr; Mike Eliason: 33tr;
James Bell Ford Library 6b; iStock 9tl, 21tr, 29br, 30bl;
Photos.com: 16br, 28tl. 46bl; Reuters: 47br.
Maps on 24, 28 and 33 by Robert L. Prince.

All other images © Dorling Kindersley.
For more information see: www.dkimages.com

Discover more at
www.dk.com

Contents

North and South
Several big sled-dog races are held in Canada and the U.S. But they can also be seen in Scandinavia, southern Europe, and even South America, where the "Andirod" attracts mushers to Argentina and Chile from all over the world.

You and your fellow "mushers" have taken up the challenge to race across the rugged wilderness of Alaska and northern Canada in the bitter depths of winter. Your life depends on a specially equipped sled and a team of dogs. You are pitting yourself against the forces of nature as well as the other teams.

More than just a sport, sled-dog racing celebrates the traditional way of life and the heritage of the North's native people.

Going the distance
Long distance sled-dog races include the Iditarod, the Yukon Quest, and the Hudson Bay Quest.

5

"Mush!"
The word *mush* comes from the cry of "*Marche!*" ("Move!") used by the early French Canadian traders to get their dog teams going.

Getting going
"Mush" is now rarely heard. But the people who go "mushing" are called "mushers." Dog teams are now urged on with the commands "A'right," "Hike," or "OK!"

A deep tradition

The dogsled has played a key role in the history of northern Canada and Alaska. The Inuit and Yupik people probably first used dogs to pull sleds about 1,000 years ago. Compared to hunting on foot, the dogsleds helped them travel much farther and faster over the snow and ice, and enabled them to haul more meat back home. In return, the dogs received a portion of the spoils. This relationship continued for hundreds of years.

European explorers, trappers, hunters, and traders spread north and west across the region from the 1700s onward. They quickly learned from the native peoples of the North that the dogsled was the best—if not the only—means of transportation throughout the freezing winter months.

Soon the sled dogs were hauling people, mail, furs, gold, and other goods to and from the forts, trading posts, and gold mines that were dotted across the Far North. By the end of the 19th century, the Canadian Northwest Mounted Police were using dogsleds in their effort to maintain law and order during the Yukon gold rush. Sleds also played an important role in the exploration of the Arctic and Antarctic in the early 20th century.

Mushing mailman
Each winter from 1910 to 1949, Percy DeWolfe took mail by dogsled to cities in the Yukon and Alaska—a round trip of 210 miles (338 km).

A GENTLEMAN travelling in a DOG CARIOLE in HUDSON'S BAY, with an INDIAN GUIDE.

Europeans traveling by dogsled in the 1820s

7

AAS centennial
In March 2008, the All-Alaska Sweepstakes was run again to celebrate its 100th anniversary. The entry fee for each musher included an ounce (31 g) of gold, and the winner-take-all prize was $100,000.

In the early 1900s, in isolated gold-rush boomtowns such as Nome, Alaska, mushing became a popular pastime each winter when gold-mining operations were shut down during the freeze-up. It became a recognized sport in 1908, when the Nome Kennel Club held the All-Alaska Sweepstakes (or AAS)—the first organized long-distance sled-dog race. Although the 408-mile (657 km) course was grueling, and the prize money was small, the race

The start of the 1912 All-Alaska Sweepstakes

proved extremely popular and it was run each year until 1917.

There were other sled-dog races throughout the North, but as gold mining waned and the population dwindled, the number of races reduced, too. At the same time, other kinds of mushing were also disappearing. By the 1960s, cars, airplanes, and snowmobiles had largely replaced the dogsled for transportation, and mushing had almost died out as part of the Northern way of life.

Then racing came to the rescue. The famous Iditarod was founded in 1973, the AAS was held again in 1983 to celebrate its 75th anniversary, and many other races followed. Mushing now thrives in North America, and is Alaska's official state sport.

Motorized
Many people replaced their dogs with snowmobiles, only to find that snowmobiles can break down or run out of fuel!

Olympics
Sled-dog racing was included as a demonstration sport in the 1932 Winter Olympics, held in Lake Placid.

Dogs and sleds

Pulling a sled through snow, ice, and blizzards demands special qualities. Sled dogs come in many shapes and sizes, but they all have strength, stamina, and a warm coat. The Canadian Inuit dog, or *qimmiq* (KIM-mik), probably became the first sled dog more than a thousand years ago. These dogs may not be directly descended from wolves, but they have certainly been crossbred with wolves at times. They almost died out in the 1960s, but are making a comeback. The qimmiq is now the official animal symbol of the Canadian territory of Nunavut.

The Alaskan malamute is another ancient Northern sled dog with great strength. But lighter, faster dogs were needed for racing. Siberian huskies were imported for the All-Alaska Sweepstakes, and they quickly dominated the race.

Over the last hundred years, the Northern dog types have been interbred and mixed with other, faster breeds to produce the ideal sled dog—the Alaskan husky. Although it is not recognized as a true breed, it is now the type of dog most commonly used for sled racing.

Chinook
The Chinook sled dog is named after the husky-mastiff cross that established this new breed in the 1920s.

Leonhard Seppala
An avid racer, "Sepp" developed the Seppala Siberian husky, a sled dog that has since become a separate breed.

For many centuries, the Northern native people used toboggans and sleds to travel across the snow.

The toboggan is made of thin planks bent upward at the front. It rides easily over soft snow and can be narrow enough to fit within a trail made by snowshoes when it is pulled by hand.

The traditional Inuit sled, or *komatik* (koh-MAH-tik), has two narrow runners with well-spaced slats between them. The komatik runs best on ice or hard-packed snow.

Native origin
Toboggan comes from the word *tobâkun*, which means "hand sled" in the Algonquin language of the Micmac people of eastern Canada.

Edible sled
In the past, sleds were held together with strips of hide. The sleds had to be stored out of reach of the dogs, who would chew them apart.

European traders and travelers in eastern Canada adopted the toboggan as a way to transport goods, and added a protective cover of animal hide so that people could travel in relative comfort. This kind of toboggan was called a cariole (cah-ree-OHL).

During the Yukon and Alaskan gold rushes of the mid- to late 1800s, basket sleds were used on harder snow and ice. This type of sled has runners, like a komatik, but the slats on which the load is carried are parallel to the runners and are raised well above the snow. This design is the model for modern sprint and mid-distance racing sleds.

Dogs to the Pole
Norwegian explorer Roald Amundsen learned about dog sledding from the native people of northern Canada. This helped him become the first person to reach the South Pole in 1911.

Hauling a toboggan

13

Handlebar: The musher holds on here.

Footboards: The musher stands on these nonslip boards on the runners.

Brake: Pressing down on the brake pushes metal studs into the snow to slow the sled.

Runners: The sled is supported on these skis, which slide over the snow.

Tail-dragger
In 2004, famed musher Jeff King introduced the tail-dragger sled. The musher stands or sits in the middle of the runners instead of standing at the tail end. These sleds have become popular in long-distance races.

First plastic
In the 1940s the Canadian police started applying bakelite, an early form of plastic, to their runners to reduce friction. This was later replaced by slip-on plastic covers.

The sled that is now usually used for long-distance races combines the qualities of the toboggan and the komatik and is called a raised toboggan sled (shown above). Like a basket sled, it has runners, but it also has a raised flat plastic bed that rides easily over softer snow. The musher stands on runners at the back.

Sled bag: *A heavy-duty nylon bag protects the load*

Brushbow: *This acts as a bumper to deflect obstacles on the trail.*

Pulling points: *A long rope, or gangline, attaches the dogs to the front of the runners.*

Cargo bed: *The load rests here.*

In the last 20 years, wood and traditional construction have given way to the use of ultra-modern materials. These super-light products include high-grade aluminum, Kevlar, carbon fiber, and epoxy resins. They produce much lighter and stronger sleds that perform better on the trail.

Snow hook This two-pronged anchor digs into the snow to keep the sled and team stationary.

Catherine Pinard
Hard work and effort made Catherine's dreams come true. She had to learn how dogs think and act, as well as how to race and care for them.

Changing direction
Cries of "Gee" and "Haw" are used to turn the team to the right and to the left.

Teamwork!

For Catherine Pinard, it all started when she was a young girl, living in Quebec—with no dogs. "I was 10 years old when I saw a film about dogsledding. And I started dreaming, imagining that I could do just that: Drive a dogsled in the North…"

Catherine Pinard never forgot that dream. Fifteen years later, in the Yukon, she made it come true

Husky sled dogs relax in their kennel. As with Catherine Pinard's dogs, their different personalities make for good teamwork.

when she competed in her first race.

At first, Catherine trained other people's dogs. Then she built a kennel, and started acquiring dogs of her own. She knew every one of her dogs personally— not just their names, but also their characters, their likes and dislikes, and the ways they worked best in the team. Some dogs like to lead, others prefer to be farther back. Some dogs are good at finding their way through fresh snow. For a race, it's important to put together a team that has the right mix of strengths to suit the conditions on the trail.

After several short races, Catherine and her team entered the Yukon Quest, which she completed twice. She later became the first woman to win the Percy DeWolfe Race.

Lifeline
Safety-conscious mushers wear a short rope that connects them to the sled so they don't get left behind if they fall off.

Mailman memorial
The 210-mile (338 km) annual Percy DeWolfe Memorial Mail Race commemorates the mailman's many round-trip journeys between Dawson in the Yukon and Eagle in Alaska.

Picket line
To keep the dogs under control before they are hitched up, mushers tether them to a securely fixed cable known as a picket line, which has a "drop line" for each dog.

Dog box
Mushers transport their dogs to races in a specially built, multi-story kennel that fits onto the bed of a truck.

Training begins when a pup is just a few months old and it can be put in a small harness. Gradually, the pup is taught to move forward on command and to stop when the musher calls "Whoa." Soon it is ready to practice in a small team, which often includes its mother, and it learns from the more experienced members of the team. Dogs are ready to compete in short races when they are one or two years old.

In the summer, when there is no snow on the ground, the dogs pull a wheeled cart to keep fit. The level of training increases through the fall. Then, during the winter months, as a big race approaches, the dogs regularly run 50–100 miles (80–160 km) to build up their fitness and stamina. Mushers and other people who care for the dogs pay attention to the animals' health,

No hands
Controlling a sled pulled by a team of dogs is very different from driving a carriage drawn by horses. On a dogsled, there are no reins!

High priority
Aliy Zirkle, the first woman to win the Yukon Quest, says that in a long-distance race the important thing is to finish with a happy, healthy, strong dog team.

making sure the dogs' feet are not sore and their muscles are not stiff.

More and more mushers are achieving success by treating their dogs as high-performance athletes. The animals are given top-quality nutrition, a well-planned training routine, and plenty of care and encouragement.

When pulling a sled, the dogs usually run in pairs. They are connected to the sled by a gangline—a long rope to which each dog is attached by a neckline.

Dogs in different positions on the gangline have different jobs to do. The two in front are the lead dogs. They must be fast and experienced and must set the pace by listening to the musher's commands. Behind them are the swing, or point, dogs, who help "swing" the sled around bends on the trail. The two at the back are the wheel dogs. They need to be strong to control the sled on tight turns.

The musher steers the team and the sled by calling out instructions to the responsive dogs, by using the brake when necessary, and by leaning to one side or the other to help the sled turn.

Spare pairs
In order to form a team of 14 dogs, you need many more to choose from. Some will be too young, some will still be in training, and some may be past their racing prime.

Firm connection
A strong, safe carabiner connects the gangline securely to the sled.

Iditarod Trail

It was January 1925. The gold-rush camp of Nome, Alaska, was now a quiet town of 1,500 people, and Dr. Curtis Welch of the U.S. Public Health Service was very worried.

A child had diphtheria, a highly contagious disease, and two Inuit children had died a few days earlier with the same symptoms. If this became an epidemic, hundreds of people would die, but there was no way to get the serum to vaccinate the townspeople. The serum could be brought by railroad to Nenana, 674 miles (1,085 km) from Nome. But there was no airplane to bring it from Nenana across the treacherous, frozen terrain to Nome.

Valiant sled dogs and their brave mushers came to the rescue. Twenty dog teams worked in relays to complete what became known as the Nome Serum Run. In temperatures that dipped to –40°F (–40°C), they carried the precious package to Nome in a little more than five days. Balto, the lead dog on the last leg, became a national hero. And there were other heroes in that race against time, including musher Leonhard Seppala and his lead dog, Togo.

Nome today
Nome, Alaska's oldest major city, was incorporated on April 9, 1901. The population topped 20,000 in 1909, but is now around 3,500.

Seppala and his team covered 260 miles (418 km).

"Iditarod" Derived from an Athabaskan word meaning "distant place," Iditarod is a small town that gave its name to the trail.

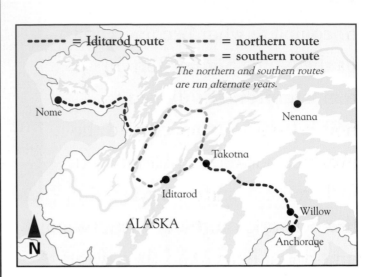

------ = Iditarod route   ------ = northern route
                            ------ = southern route

The northern and southern routes are run alternate years.

Nome

Nenana

Takotna

Iditarod

ALASKA

Willow

Anchorage

N

Steak for all! Villages along the trail compete to offer the best hospitality. Takotna gives a steak dinner to mushers who stay there for the 24-hour layover.

By the early 1970s, dog-sledding —as a means of transportation, as a sport, and as a part of native culture—looked as if it might disappear. Fortunately, a group of mushers in Alaska refused to let this happen. In 1973, they scraped together $50,000 in prize money and organized a race to run 1,150 miles (1,850 km) along the historic Iditarod Trail from Anchorage to Nome, commemorating the Nome Serum Run. The race was a huge success, and the Iditarod Trail Sled Dog Race has been run every year since then. It is now the largest sporting event in Alaska.

The race starts on the first Saturday in March each year, and the winner usually completes the course in nine days. Mushers make three rest stops along the route. The first of these is a 24-hour layover that is usually taken between 300 and 600 miles (480 and 960 km) into the race.

Junior Iditarod
Every year there is also a race for mushers under the age of 18. It is run over a course of 160 miles (257 km) on the weekend before the Iditarod.

Dogs rest on hay to keep dry.

It's noisy, colorful, and exciting on Fourth Avenue in Anchorage, Alaska, on the first Saturday in March. Hundreds of spectators throng the sidewalks, huddled in thick parkas to protect against the

Iditariders
On the trip from Anchorage to Eagle River, each musher carries a lucky passenger who pays for the privilege. The money helps fund the race.

Pick a number
The starting order is determined by drawing numbers from a boot. The mushers pick their numbers in the order they signed up for the race.

cold, while up to 75 dogsled teams exuberantly await the ceremonial start of the Iditarod. The air is filled with loud, excited barking and the raised voices of the mushers, as the dogs leap and strain at their harnesses, raring to go.

The teams depart at two-minute intervals, winding their way out of town toward Eagle River, 25 miles (40 km) away.

The next day, the race begins in earnest at Willow, on the Iditarod Trail itself. From now on, it's up to each musher to make the best possible time, while keeping all the dogs healthy, well nourished, and sufficiently rested.

Who knows what the race will throw at them? Gale-force winds, white-out blizzards, plummeting temperatures—the competitors must be ready for anything.

Common time
To make the race fair, the differences between the teams' starting times are balanced out by adjusting the time each team spends at the 24-hour stop.

Consolation
A lit red lantern hangs at the finish line, and the last musher to cross the line puts it out. He or she receives the Red Lantern Trophy.

Yukon Quest

Mighty Yukon
The Yukon River is 2,300 miles (3,700 km) long and drains an area larger than Alberta or Texas.

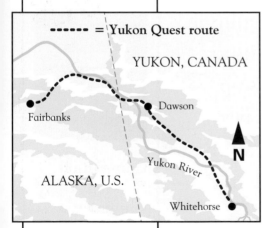

- - - - - = Yukon Quest route

YUKON, CANADA

Fairbanks

Dawson

Yukon River

N

ALASKA, U.S.

Whitehorse

Yukon trail
This map shows the trail used by the long, freezing, and difficult Yukon Quest sled-dog race.

Known as "the toughest sled-dog race in the world," the Yukon Quest was dreamed up by a group of mushers and historians in the Bull's Eye Saloon, in Fairbanks, Alaska, in 1983. They imagined a race that would follow the trail taken by prospectors to reach the interior of Alaska during the 1898 gold rush. The race would be named after the mighty Yukon River, the old "highway of the North." The organizers shared a vision to dedicate the race to the gold seekers, mail carriers, trappers, and traders who settled the North in the early 1900s.

In February 1984, their plan became reality when 26 teams set off from Fairbanks to race more than 1,000 miles (1,600 km) to the town

Up and down
The race is run in opposite directions in alternate years, starting in Fairbanks in even-numbered years and in Whitehorse in odd-numbered years.

of Whitehorse in the Canadian Yukon Territory in the depths of the Arctic winter. Despite the bitter weather and a very testing route, only six teams dropped out, and the winner made it to Whitehorse in exactly 12 days.

Dawson Award
The first musher to reach Dawson City, who then goes on to complete the race, gets more than 4 ounces (124 g) of Yukon gold!

In 2006, the Yukon Quest nearly turned deadly. In the darkest hours of the night, three mushers and their teams were caught in a sudden snow storm on Eagle Summit at an altitude of 3,650 ft (1,100 m). They had lost the trail and were trying to make their way down the steep mountainside. One of the teams suddenly dashed forward.

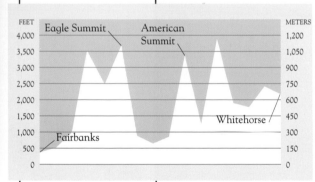

Musher Randy Chappel clung to the lurching sled but was thrown off and his team disappeared into the dark. The other dogs led all three mushers to the next checkpoint, and when the storm cleared, the missing dog team was airlifted out by helicopter. That time, mushers and dogs were unharmed, but the Quest had shown how risky it could be.

Elevation extremes
The Yukon Quest involves some steep climbs as well as fast, level sections along the ice of the Yukon River.

What makes the Yukon Quest so tough? Mainly, it's the treacherous terrain. The route goes through the harsh vastness of the Arctic landscape, traversing four high mountain passes and several frozen rivers. The race also takes place in the coldest part of winter, and the mushers spend much of the time in true wilderness conditions. The Yukon Quest has only eight checkpoints, making this a true test of survival for dogs and mushers.

Silver run
In 2008, the Yukon Quest celebrated a quarter-century of history when the 25th race was held.

Hudson Bay Quest

Big white Churchill, Canada, is known as the "polar bear capital of the world." Every fall these giants pass nearby on their way to the sea-ice of Hudson Bay.

Founded in 2004, the Canadian Hudson Bay Quest is a 250-mile (400 km) sled-dog race between Churchill in Manitoba and Arviat in Nunavut, across the frozen tundra near Hudson Bay. Although it is much shorter than the Iditarod and the Yukon Quest, this is a race with a difference. While food awaits the teams at checkpoints along the routes of the other two races, mushers on the Hudson Bay Quest must carry all their own provisions. In an emergency, food is available at Nunalla, a rest stop halfway along the trail, but you receive an eight-hour penalty if you use it. To protect against the elements, every musher must carry a tent as well as a cold-weather sleeping bag.

This adventure in self-sufficient dogsledding attracts mushers anxious to keep Canada's dogsledding traditions alive. Many Inuit mushers participate, and some teams use the low, wide komatik sled, which has advantages on hard and uneven snow.

The route of the race changes slightly each year according to the conditions.

Stay in touch
Mushers are often far from help in difficult conditions. They must carry a global positioning system (GPS) and satellite phone.

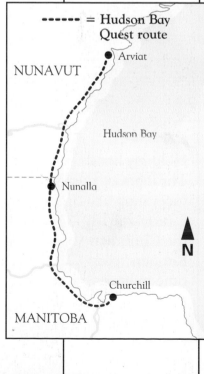

------ = Hudson Bay Quest route

NUNAVUT

Arviat

Hudson Bay

Nunalla

Churchill

MANITOBA

N

Close company
After spending
a night on
the snow-
covered ice,
Hudson Bay
Quest musher
Miriam Koerner
discovered
fresh polar
bear tracks!

Helping hands
Throughout the
race, support
is provided by
the Canadian
Rangers, part-
time military
reservists based
in remote
communities.

For the spectators waiting at the Hudson Bay Quest finish line, the tension is unbearable. The second half of this race has been grueling. Hudson Bay is notorious for its blizzards, and this year the mushers have been hit by driving snow as they've made their way over rough and jagged sea ice to avoid the slush at the mouths of the frozen rivers.

No driver may ask for help, food, or shelter unless he or she is pulling out of the race. But competitors are allowed to help each other. There have been many times when a

musher has risked losing the race in order to aid another.

Today, there's a white-out and several teams have had to give up. Whose team will be the first to appear from the swirling snow?

Harking back
In keeping with the sport's origins, each musher racing from Arviat to Churchill carries an animal fur to "trade" with a Parks Canada representative at the end of the race.

What's a white-out?
It's when the snow is so thick in the air that it's hard to see through it.

Major expense
Booties are worn during training and racing. A dog team goes through several thousand of them in a single season.

Big meals
The combined weight of a team's food-drop packages can be as much as 2,000 pounds (900 kg). The dogs need lots of protein, so they eat large amounts of meat, fish, and animal fat.

Behind the scenes

Preparations for these big races begin long before race day. In addition to the intense training in the months before the competition, each musher must gather all the items that the race rules require. These items are necessary to ensure the survival of the driver and the health and safety of the dogs. They include a cold-weather sleeping bag, a hand ax, snowshoes, a cooker and fuel (used to melt snow for the dogs to drink and to heat up their frozen food), and eight booties for each dog in the team. These booties protect the dogs' feet by preventing the buildup of snow between their toes. All this equipment must be packed on the sled, and it is all checked by marshals before, during, and after the race.

Before the Iditarod and Yukon Quest, the drivers must also deliver adequate food for the dog teams and themselves, carefully packaged and labeled, well in advance of the race. These "food drops" are then flown out by bush plane to the checkpoints along the route, ready for the arrival of the teams. Food-drop bags also include extra equipment such as harnesses, ganglines, batteries, clothing, and parts for the sled.

Ticket home
In the Iditarod, the sled must be capable of hauling any injured or tired dogs under a cover, so they can be brought safely to the finish.

How many dogs?
Each race has its own rules about the maximum number of dogs in a team at the start and the minimum number at the finish.

Inukshuk
These traditional stone markers have guided the Inuit for centuries. Today, fluorescent markers are used to guide mushers along the race trails.

Before and during the races, hundreds of volunteers are involved in making sure the events run smoothly. On the Iditarod and Yukon Quest, snowmobile riders drive along the whole course to groom the trail, so that the first teams don't have the difficult task of breaking through fresh snow. Thousands of handmade fluorescent

and reflective markers are then placed along the trail to show the way.

Throughout the race, marshals are posted at each of the checkpoints to check the teams in and out, and to make sure that each musher is carrying all the required items. Emergency services are on hand, too, to deal with injury or illness, and to search for lost racers. Veterinarians with specialized knowledge of sled dogs examine all the dogs before the race and at all the checkpoints. If any animal is considered unfit it is taken out of the race. Some checkpoints are designated as "dog drops. " Mushers can choose to remove dogs from the teams at these locations, but once a dog has been dropped, it can't be brought back into the team.

Snow birds
The bush pilots who deliver the food drops are always on call in case of emergency.

Veteran vet
Evan Fisk is the race vet for the Hudson Bay Quest. He checks dogs at the checkpoint and makes their well-being a priority.

Winning woman
In 1985, Libby Riddles became the first woman to win the Iditarod. She gained the lead by heading out during a snowstorm.

Veteran musher
Mary Shields was the first woman to complete the Iditarod. This was in 1974. Mary still keeps sled dogs and has written books about her experiences.

Supermushers

It was March 2007. Dave Monson watched from above as his 11-year-old daughter, Tekla, drove her sled down a steep descent to a frozen river. All went well until the team turned sharply, sending Tekla spinning off the sled and across the ice. Dave saw the dogs head down the river and heard his daughter call after them. To his amazement, the lead dogs looked back, turned the team in a long curve, and returned to Tekla, who was kneeling on the ice.

In a remarkable endeavor for one so young, Tekla was running a 700-mile (1,125 km) section of the Iditarod Trail in memory of her mother, the legendary Susan Butcher.

Susan made her mark on this great race by winning it four times—in 1986, '87, '88, and '90. Her successes brought dogsledding to the attention of the world, and her enthusiasm and perseverance attracted many more women to a sport that had, until then, been largely dominated by men.

Teenage racer
In 2004, 12 days after she turned 18, Ellie Claus became the youngest woman ever to complete the Iditarod.

Many of Susan's fans were in Nome to give an emotional welcome

to her plucky daughter as she reached the finish line of the race that her mother had dominated for so long.

Susan Butcher (above and below)

41

On February 20, 2007, the amazing team of Lance Mackey and his dogs crossed the Yukon Quest finish line to win the race in a record-breaking time of 10 days, 2 hours, and 37 minutes. This was Lance's third consecutive Yukon Quest win—a great achievement by any standard, but particularly remarkable given that he had undergone surgery for cancer in 2001 and had been unable to race for two years. Then, just three weeks later, Lance went on to win the Iditarod, too. He was the first person ever to do this—a feat that no one had thought possible. This supermusher amazed people again when he repeated this double win in 2008, with many of the same dogs.

Another supermusher, Hans Gatt—who has conquered the Yukon Quest three times—came in second in 2007. Born in Austria, Hans now lives in British Columbia, and in 2002 he became the first European to win the Yukon Quest. Hans designs and builds high-tech racing sleds that are used by many of the world's top mushers.

Youngest ever
Dallas Seavey is the youngest musher to compete in and finish the Iditarod. Dallas ran the race in 2005, just one day after turning 18— a hard record to beat.

Hans Gatt

Blind courage
In 2006, Rachael Scdoris completed the Iditarod despite being legally blind. A "visual interpreter" went ahead and relayed information about the trail by two-way radio.

Jeff King has been dubbed the "Winningest Musher in the World." He has been racing since 1980 and has won 30 Alaskan races, including one Yukon Quest and four Iditarods. He estimates he has driven more than 100,000 miles (160,000 km) on a dog sled! Jeff has a reputation as a "mad inventor." In addition to the tail-dragger sled, he has created a hand-warming device for his handlebar.

Jeff King

Leonhard Seppala, the Nome Serum Run hero, was probably the most remarkable musher of his time, winning three All-Alaska Sweepstakes

in a row. His dogs were used as transportation throughout the year, running on snow in winter and pulling a handcar on the tracks of the Alaskan Kougarok Railway in summer. All told, he estimated that in 1917 his team covered some 7,000 miles (11,250 km).

Helping hand
In the 2004 Hudson Bay Quest, Inuit musher David Oolooyak (above) won the race despite turning back to help his friend Phillip Kigusiutnak, whose dog team had broken away on the trail.

You can do it, too

Mushing is a sport for young people, too, and not only in the far North. Junior races take place every year throughout the colder parts of Canada and the United States, including New England and Montana.

Dogsledding doesn't have to be competitive. Many people in Canada and the U.S. head off into the frozen landscape to enjoy the thrill of recreational sledding with family and friends. If you don't have

Nature trail
Dogsledding is a great way to see the wildlife in winter, as well as the stunning scenery.

your own dogs, mushing excursions led by expert drivers will whisk you along backcountry trails, through snowy forests, across glaciers, and over frozen rivers for a few hours, a day, or even a week. Sometimes, you can drive the team yourself.

No snow
In some places where there isn't snow, mushers compete by harnessing their dog teams to specially designed carts.

For the people in this book, taking part in dogsledding was a dream. Through their own effort and determination, they made their dreams come true. Perhaps you can, too!

Glossary

Blizzard
A severe snowstorm with violent winds. During a blizzard, strong winds pick up fine snow lying on the ground and hurl it through the air.

Boomtown
A place that was built up very quickly following the nearby discovery of gold or other valuable resources.

Carbon fiber
A very strong but lightweight material.

Diphtheria
A disease of the lungs that is easily passed from person to person.

Epidemic
An outbreak of disease that spreads rapidly through a community.

Excursions
Trips or journeys.

Exuberant
Very enthusiastic or excited.

Gangline
A long rope to which each sled dog is attached by a neckline.

Global Positioning System (GPS)
A navigation system that uses satellites orbiting the Earth to pinpoint the exact location of a person to within a few feet (m).

Gold rush
The movement of large numbers of people to an area where gold has been discovered.

Grueling
Very long and difficult.

Inuit and Yupik
Native peoples of the Arctic.

Inukshuk
A traditional stone trail marker used by Inuit people.

Komatik
An early type of sled.

Marshal
Person who helps to control a dogsled race, and makes sure all the rules are followed by competitors.

Mushers
Drivers of sleds pulled by sled dogs.

Qimmiq
The Canadian Inuit sled dog and official animal symbol of Nunavut.

Parka
A type of heavy jacket with a hood, designed to protect the body and face against wind and freezing conditions.

Plummeting
Falling very fast and dramatically.

Provisions
Essential supplies, especially food.

Recreational
A sport or hobby that's done just for fun, not as part of a competition.

Remote
Located out of the way, far from other people.

Runners
The long, thin metal or wooden blades of a sled that are in direct contact with the snow.

Satellite phone
A telephone that can send and receive signals to and from satellites orbiting the Earth.

Self-sufficient
Able to survive alone and without help.

Serum
A liquid that is used to protect people against a disease.

Stamina
The strength and ability to do something for a long period of time.

Summit
The very top, usually of a mountain.

Trapper
A person who lays traps to catch animals, usually for their fur and meat.

Vaccinate
To give a medication that helps protect against a particular disease.